MARKET SEGMENTATION IN THE FMCG INDUSTRY

Mark Freeman

Market Segmentation Is the foundation of all business strategies

Printed in the United States of America

First Printing: February 2020

ISBN 9798604794708

CONTENTS

INTRODUCTION

Welcome to Market segmentation in the FMCG Industry. This book was last updated in 2020 and is a comprehensive guide on how to gather data, performing and implementing market segmentation in top-tier Fast Moving Consumer Goods (FMCG) companies.

Market segmentation is the art of subdividing a market into homogeneous subsets of consumers, where any subset may conceivably be selected as a target group to be reached with a distinct marketing mix.

A company that knows the industry and its consumers better than everyone else creates strong durable competitive advantages. Successful marketing professionals focus on being the central role in strategic and consumer-centric thinking. Marketing starts with a thorough understanding of the market.

Consumer-centricity is the number one success factor in the FMCG industry.

ABOUT THIS BOOK

The goal of market segmentation is to offer the right products, in the right locations to the right consumers.

This book was written to give readers a hands-on understanding of how market segmentation is performed in practice. This book serves as a guide for readers wanting to implement actionable and consumer-centric marketing strategies via market segmentation.

This book takes marketing strategies to the next level by outlining how to understand your consumers better than anyone else. Offer relevant products and marketing messages to the right consumers and turn consumer insights into action.

This is a comprehensive step-by-step guide that takes the reader through the process of how to work with market segmentation in the FMCG industry.

All steps have been thoroughly evaluated and successfully implemented in practice. The knowledge shared in this book has been accumulated by working in the industry for years and from extensive research on the subject.

Market Segmentation in the FMCG Industry

- Define the market: Volume and profit pool calculations
- Why market segmentation is relevant and the objectives
- Levels of market intelligence and how to utilize different datasets

- Design a consumer segmentation research study for psychographic and need states data

- Market segmentation models and how to use them

- Full implementation of the market segmentation and how to make it actionable

THE MARKETING ROLE

Marketing professionals around the world contribute to the financial success of the enterprise they work in by having a solid understanding of its customer base and the market dynamics. Through this understanding and insights about the market, marketeers develop and deliver products and value propositions that best serve the consumers' needs and desires. Successful marketing professionals focus on being the central role in strategic planning.

Marketing professionals are often tempted to focus on mass marketing activities and building brand awareness in general. It has become more about pushing out generic messages and products to consumers for short-term sales, instead of building brand loyalty and long-term value creation.

Marketing professionals can also be tempted to fall into being a support function for other departments in the company. This creates a negative spiral where the company slowly but surely drift away from being relevant for its customers. It is of essence today that a successful marketing professional instead focuses on being the central role in strategy and consumer-centric thinking. Market segmentation is essential for consumer understanding and the foundation for all marketing strategies.

Market Segmentation is a Process of
- Define the market
- Understand the needs of different consumer groups (Segments) within the market
- Determine the value proposition to meet consumer needs
- Communicate and deliver these value propositions to the right target group in the right locations
- Monitor the development and course-correct where necessary

DEFINE THE MARKET

Part 1
The beginning

SIZE OF THE MARKET

The very first step of any market segmentation starts with an assessment of the total size of the market in terms of total volumes and profit pool. Complete knowledge of volume and profits generates opportunities for a company to pursue higher profit-building activities. A lack of knowledge can lead to blind spots in a company's strategic vision or that the company is being trapped in areas of weak or fading profitability.

In this section, we describe a useful framework for the analysis of how volumes and profits are distributed across the industry. A thorough analysis of the size of the market provides a company with a rich understanding of the industry's profit structure. This is what we call volume and profit pool.

Every company has its own approach dependent on industry specifics and country of origin, but the framework remains the same across countries, industries and companies.

Volume Pool

An assessment of the volume pool is, in theory, a very straightforward exercise. While the goal is simple, achieving it can be more complicated. Data is far from perfect in most companies. Data needs to be structured on channels, brands and products for the volume pool. The assessment is therefore often done through multiple data sources. The company needs to be pragmatic and use the best available information at hand. Qualified estimates are needed for areas with no or little data.

An FMCG company should at least know how much is being shipped to its customers every month. Shipment volumes are normally widely available in the organization. Some companies also know how much its competitors are shipping every month, which makes it easier to assess the total volume pool.

It is also not uncommon for a company to have access to several different data sources as the shipment volumes often go through many different types of trade channels (For example online and offline). It is, therefore, necessary to add them together to calculate the percentage of the total volumes that the different trade channels stand for. The better information you have at hand, the better the assessment will be.

If you only know your company's share of the market (SOM) in some channels, use it as a proxy to determine the total volumes for your competitors in the other channels.

Label	Shipment Volumes	Competitors	Total Industry Volumes	SOM %
Traditional Trade	7,000,000	50,000,000	57,000,000	12.30%
Online Trade	2,000,000	?	?	?
Direct to Consumers (DTC)	1,000,000	?	?	?
Estimated Online Trade	2,000,000	14,260,162.60	16,260,162.60	12.30%
Estimated DTC	1,000,000	7,130,081.30	8,130,081.30	12.30%
Grand Total	10,000,000	71,390,243.90	81,390,243.90	12.30%

The industry volumes for Online and DTC are calculated by dividing the company's shipment volumes in the trade channel with a SOM proxy. In this case, we use 12.3% which is the same as in the traditional trade channel. This gives us the total industry volumes. Competitor volumes are estimated by subtracting the industry volumes with the company's own shipment volumes.

These calculations give us a basic approximation of the total volume pool. A more sophisticated way of determining SOM per channel can be done via a qualitative approach, where the company assesses its relative strength per trade channel internally. Another way to determine the relative strength of the company is through a quantitative research study.

Once the volume pool has been estimated, it is time to determine the profit pool. The profit pool requires a bit more work since we need detailed information about our competitors.

Profit Pool

Brand Volumes

In order to know the profit pool of the market, the volume pool needs to be broken down on at least brand level to reflect the different price points in the market. Again, the better information you have at hand, the more accurate the profit pool will be. The brand volumes for competitors are estimated through the same approach as we did for the industry volumes.

Retail Selling Price

Once the volumes for the major brands have been calculated, it is time to look at the retail sales prices (RSP) in the market. This piece of information is often very well known, since it is public data. Stock keeping Units (SKU) that have similar price points within a brand can be aggregated. Brands that have different price levels need to be broken down into several sub-brands within the brand family.

Once we have the retail sales price for the brands, we can easily calculate the Gross Sales, by multiplying RSP with the volumes for each brand/sub-family.

Gross Sales = Total Units sold x Sales Price per Units

Net Sales

Net Sales is what remains when all returns, allowances and discounts have been subtracted from Gross Sales. Net Sales is primarily used to analyze the company's revenues, growth and operational expenses. In some industries, taxes are also deducted in this step.

Net Sales = Gross sales– Sales Returns- Allowances - Discounts

Gross Margin

The next step of the process is to determine the gross margin per brand. In order to calculate the Gross Margin (GM), we need to understand the production cost for different brands and products. This information should be very well known for the company's own products, but estimations are required for competitor products. The most straightforward way of doing this is to assume the same production cost for comparable competitor products. A way to improve the accuracy is to also consider the scale of operations for competing products and slightly adjusting it up or down based on own market experience.

Analyzing the Profit Pool

Once the profit pool is completed, we can start to analyze the results. The information should cover most brands in the market. The weighted average price (WAP) in the market can be calculated by an aggregation of the total sales value and divide it by the total sales volumes in the market. This is a very useful KPI and enables the company to track the overall price development in the market.

Brands with similar price points can be aggregated together to form different price segments in the market. This gives the company knowledge about the WAP development for different price segments. In addition to share of market in volumes, we can also look at the share of value for each brand and segment.

A good way to visualize the findings is by looking at the total volume and the GM development over time in the market. We can display the GM % per price segment to get a thorough understanding of what is driving the volumes and profitability.

A small volume segment in terms of volumes can often show up as highly profitable niche opportunities once we also have information about sales value and GM contribution at hand.

Size of the Overall Market

Once we have the volume pool and profit pool, we have come a long way in the assessment of the potential in the market. We know how much value the company can generate and the current total demand. This information is critical for the market segmentation process. Historical data should be saved so the company can forecast future market demand and GM contribution.

The profit pool will be plugged into the market segmentation model that we will cover in the following chapters. A company can with this information assign volumes and profitability numbers to the consumer segments that are identified via the market segmentation model. It will allow the company to determine if the underlying demand and consumer needs that can be filled in the market are profitable opportunities for the company.

Some segments might be bigger than others, but the company needs to make a strategic decision if it should pursue higher volume opportunities through the economy of scale or go into the more profitable segments in the market. This decision should be decided by the management team in the company.

A company also needs to assess its competitive strengths and how to stretch its brand portfolio across multiple consumer segments. More about the segmentation later, but this decision is imperative for the future success of the company.

FRAME THE NEEDS OF YOUR CONSUMERS

Part 2
Mapping the market

CONSUMER NEEDS AND DESIRES

To truly understand the needs and desires of consumers requires insights about the market. A company cannot simply ask what kind of product the consumers want or to follow what other companies are doing. To gain a deeper understanding of the market, a company needs to truly understand the need states and motivational factors of the consumers. The qualitative research is the foundation for this process.

Market segmentation is all about dividing the market into different segments and look for identical benefits. A company should focus on the most promising segments in the market.

Segmentation assumes that a market is heterogeneous and not homogeneous in nature. A homogenous market refers to a situation where buyers of products are found to be uniform in their needs, habits and choices. When a company uses the same marketing message nationwide, this is the assumption of the market. A heterogeneous market is the opposite and refers to a situation where buyers are different in their needs, habits and choices.

The essence of market segmentation is to divide the market into smaller consumer groups having certain homogenous characteristics. It could be something as simple as splitting the market by demographic variables such as income, age and gender. Consumer groups may be different not only by demographic variables but also by social class, family life, lifestyle, culture, etc.

Market segmentation is the art of subdividing a market into homogeneous subsets of consumers, where any subset may conceivably be selected as a target group to be reached with a distinct marketing mix.

Objectives of Market Segmentation

- Grouping consumers based on their homogeneous characteristics
- Identify needs, taste preferences and buying motivation
- Facilitate market strategies, targets & goals of the company
- Ensure market activities of a company is consumer-centric
- Identify areas where new consumer demand may be created and where market areas can be expanded
- Identify gaps in the market and new market opportunities

The main purpose is to prepare separate marketing programs and strategies for each consumer segment.

The Requirements for Each Segment

Each of segment needs to be identified as a relevant cluster in the market. Is it possible to measure the size of the segment, is the segment significant in size and accessible for the company? Is the segment homogeneous enough and deserving to be a stand-alone segment in the market?

Marketing Tactics

There are several levels of market tactics that a company can implement after the market segmentation is completed. A company can start with the traditional mass marketing strategy to build overall awareness for one of its brands. This assumes that the market is homogeneous in its preference for a brand, which is typical for ATL marketing. The brand is promoted through a national marketing program and with a generic brand message.

The next level is to differentiate a brand's product offering to specific consumer segments. Consumers do not normally accept all SKUs under the same brand family. SKUs can be adapted to fulfill the needs and motivations within the different consumer segments. It can be differentiated through flavor, color, shapes, and qualities. The purpose is to provide different product offerings to different segments. The higher the market share a brand has, the easier it is to branch it off across multiple consumer segments. There is always a limit to how far a company can stretch a brand across different segments. Once the consumer demand within the current segments is saturated, it is time for the company to launch a new brand, fulfilling different needs. The marketing department needs to make sure that brands in the portfolio do not overlap too much across the different consumer segments. If two brands fulfill the same needs and motivation, it could be time to consider a brand migration.

Target marketing defines a set of potential buyers of a product and adapts the communication message specifically to this consumer segment. The objective is to adopt a market message that speaks directly to the needs and wants of the consumer group.

The three tactical steps in market segmentation are mass marketing to build overall brand awareness. Product differentiation– and extensions to fulfill different consumer needs. Target marketing to shape the brand message directly to the target audience.

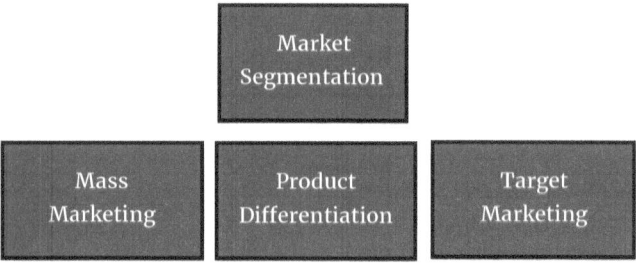

Segmentation Process

- Analyze the needs of consumers
- Analyze the motivations of consumers
- Analyze the characteristics of consumers
- Cluster consumers into suitable segments
- Formulate a marketing mix for the identified segments
- Feedback about the various segments from experts in the company
- Select the higher potential segment(s) to allocate investments in

Different Ways to Segment the Market

There are many ways to segment the market into smaller homogeneous groups. Even simple ways to segment the market provide a company with tools for more sophisticated marketing strategies. The major market segmentation methods are outlined below. A company can choose to apply some or all of them.

- Sales Segmentation
- Geographical segmentation
- Demographic segmentation
- Socioeconomic segmentation
- Psychographic segmentation
- Needs Segmentation.

LEVEL OF MARKET INTELLIGENCE

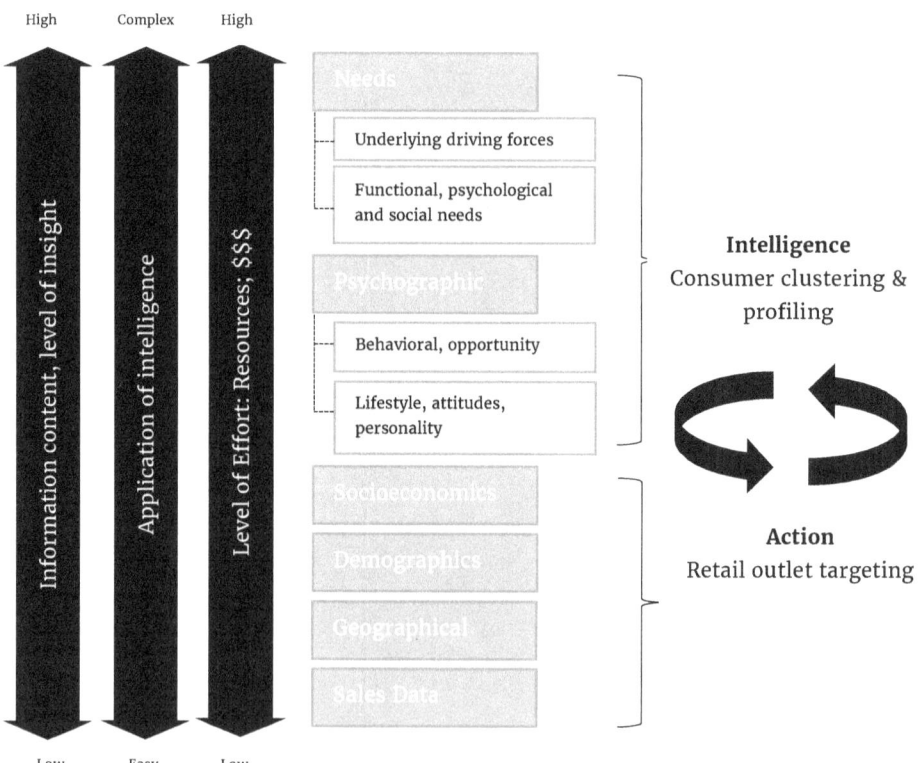

High — Complex — High

Information content, level of insight

Application of intelligence

Level of Effort: Resources; $$$

Needs
- Underlying driving forces
- Functional, psychological and social needs

Psychographic
- Behavioral, opportunity
- Lifestyle, attitudes, personality

Socioeconomics

Demographics

Geographical

Sales Data

Intelligence
Consumer clustering & profiling

Action
Retail outlet targeting

Low — Easy — Low

Sales Segmentation

One of the most straightforward and common ways of segmenting the market is by using sales data to divide the market into different segments. This is a simple, but powerful way of increasing the basic understanding of the market. Sales segmentation is often formed after the company's internal view of the market.

Sales segmentation includes looking at different price segments and divides all brands and SKUs according to their current price points. These core price segments are often named Premium, Mid-price and Value. The market WAP determines the Mid-price segment and rules are set to how far from Mid-Price a brand must be to qualify as Value or Premium brand.

Other ways of segmenting the market can be by product specifications or functionality. Products that share similar characteristics such as flavor or packaging types are often segmented together.

The advantage of this market segmentation is that a company normally has good data available and able to track the development on an ongoing basis. A company can spot gaps in the market based on what is currently selling and can replicate competitor products that trend upwards. The big downside with this approach is that the company can only see what is currently selling in the market. The company is unaware of consumer demand unless there already exists a similar product in the market. Sales segmentation can often also be quite different from how consumers navigate the market.

Sales data segmentation can quickly be implemented and used in the organization. The product portfolio of a brand can be expanded based on what is selling well. Selling additional products for a brand that is selling well today is often a relatively easy task.

Geographical Segmentation

Geographical segmentation is also a common way for a company to segment the market. Geographical segmentation can be done by dividing areas after region, states, city size, climate or density classes. Density can be defined as rural, suburban and urban areas. Geographic segmentation is also relatively simple, yet an effective method of understanding and targeting consumers within different areas.

Companies with large national or international markets can benefit from this kind of segmentation, since regions often have different needs, wants and cultural characteristics. It is not uncommon that consumers share similar characteristics based on where they live. This is also a good approach for companies with a limited budget, as it is often a low-cost approach.

The geographical segmentation is also easy to implement and communicate in an organization since it can be displayed on maps with clearly defined boundaries. Sales territories can be drawn based on this segmentation and immediate action can be taken.

Demographic Segmentation

Demographic segmentation is when a company divides the market into segments based on age, gender, religion and education, etc. Demographic variables tell a good story about consumers and their background. These variables have a high impact on consumer choice and often a good indicator of what kind of brand and SKUs a consumer would prefer. Younger consumers are very often more openminded to product innovation and news in general. Brand preferences are often formed during the younger stages of life. Gender is also a dividing factor when It comes to brands and products. It is not unusual that a brand only targets one gender.

Demographic information is often widely available and can be purchased for a relatively low cost. Implementation is also relatively simple once the demographic target has been identified. If a brand aims to target younger consumers with high education, then the marketing efforts should be focused on for example university areas. There are several examples of global brands today that have been very successful in using this type of market segmentation to increase sales. One of the downsides with only using this approach is that it is relatively easy to figure out the consumer profile a company is targeting with its marketing budget and for a competitor to replicate the success.

Socioeconomic Segmentation

Socioeconomic segmentation is when a company divides the market based on people with similar characteristics. These characteristics can be social or economic standing, level of education, current profession and ethnic background. This information is less available but can be derived by combining datasets such as geography, demographic information and sales data. Socioeconomic status significantly impacts consumer choices, beliefs and attitudes. An induvial from an affluent social class, will likely make different decisions and have more options available than others. Product purchases are often made in order to show belonging to different social classes.

Marketing efforts need to have a more subtle message and can in some cases also be more controversial than just using demographic data for targeting consumers. Socioeconomic segmentation is often used by companies selling luxury products. Retail outlets used for this type of consumer targeting are often niched to certain areas in the market.

Implementation is also more challenging since it requires combining datasets and pinpointing locations that are suitable for the target group. A well-executed socioeconomic segmentation often leads to tapping into very profitable product niches in the market with high consumer loyalty.

Psychographic Segmentation

Psychographic segmentation is when a company divides the market after prospective, current and former consumers that share similar personality traits, beliefs, values and lifestyles. Psychographic segmentation is used to describe the characteristics of consumers. All these factors have a significant impact on consumer choice and represent one of the highest levels of consumer understanding.

Identifying these segments enables powerful ways of marketing products to people that do not share the same demographic profile, geography or other easily identified characteristics. Consumers have different psychographic compositions and grouping these together is the start of an advanced consumer segmentation.

This method enables a company to market products to individuals that otherwise seem heterogeneous. A company normally discovers the need for this type of segmentation when the traditional target segments generate radically different needs and responses to a marketing message.

Every brand has its personality whether it is intentional or not. When consumers engage with a brand and can relate to the products, it creates a bond between the consumer and the brand. Learning about the personality traits for brands helps a company to refine its brand portfolio and enhance a brand personality that appeals to different consumer groups. Marketing efforts are focused at position a brand to the desired consumer personalities. Examples of brand personalities can be playful, innovative, reliable, etc.

Lifestyles are also an important factor to consider in the segmentation. Consumers have different life patterns, which includes the phases in life a consumer is in. Consumers' wants and desires change based on these patterns. Marketing efforts are then focused on providing these wants and desires of the consumers.

Attitudes are also important factors in the psychographic segmentation. Consumers view brands through the lens of the activities a company is engaging in. Promoting a brand together with other lifestyle activities boost a positive attitude toward a brand within a target group.

Gathering psychographic data is often expensive and requires a high work effort from the organization, but this kind of segmentation often yields the highest. A well-executed psychographic segmentation increases sales for a company by increased purchase frequency, loyalty and lifetime value for a brand.

The insights of the different psychographic segments need to be thoroughly communicated in the organization and to target different consumer groups requires a high level of market sophistication.

Market research is needed to gather the data for the Psychographic segmentation Gathering data and the full implementation will be outlined in the following chapters.

Needs-based Segmentation

Need-based segmentation is a powerful segmentation method that divides the market into different needs-states. This gives a deeper understanding of current, but also unmet needs in the market. A company knows what kind of products it sells, but the underlying drivers or needs it fulfills is not always fully understood. An example of a product is an energy drink. The product makes the consumers less tired but fulfills the needs differently. Some consumers need the product to keep concentration up when studying, others need it as a mixing ingredient for an alcoholic drink.

Need-based segmentation Is not only limited to functional needs, but it can also be social needs. Social needs can include the need to be part of a group or the need to be part of a community etc. Products can also trigger different psychological needs, such as stress relief, inspiration, excitement, etc.

Market efforts can be focused to deliver a need-based message that speaks directly to different consumer groups. Implementation of need-based segmentation is the same as for Psychographic segmentation.

Gathering data and the full implementation will be outlined in the following chapters.

Benefits of Market Segmentation

- Knowledge of market opportunities and market gaps
- Knowledge of consumer needs
- More effective marketing programs
- Product differentiation other than pricing
- Common internal language for consumer groups

DESIGN OF THE SEGMENTATION RESEARCH STUDY

Gathering Psychographic and Need-based Data

An important step in setting up a research study is to write a clear and concise research brief. The brief should be distributed internally and to the market research company. A good market research brief takes a little bit of extra time in the initial phase but will save time later in the process.

A good research brief should contain the following topics and be around two to three pages long. The research brief works as the steering document for the whole project.

Research Brief Content

- Purpose
- Background
- Information needed for the research
- Expected use of results
- Action standards
- Sample composition
- Methodology
- Timeline

The steps in the research project

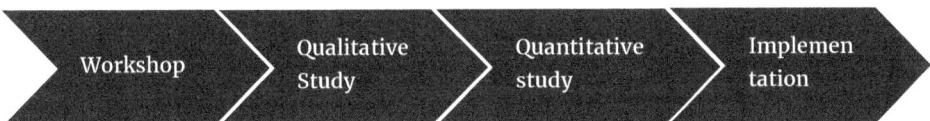

Workshop (approx. one to two weeks)

In the workshop and startup phase, the project manager should host a startup meeting where the market and research company go through what is currently known about the category and the consumers. This figures as the base in the segmentation research.

A short version of the research brief should be presented to the group and the objectives of the segmentation should be clear. The earlier key stakeholders are involved in the project, the better. The project manager should also make sure to have stakeholders that are responsible for the implementation of the market segmentation present during the meeting

The project manager should after the meeting go through the details of the project with the research company. This should cover how to arrange the focus groups and which brands that should be included in the research. A good rule of thumb is to include at least 85 percent of the market in terms of volume or sales.

Background information such as volume and profit pool should also be shared. The most important information to share with the research company is how to handle the screening process and to make sure it is nationally representative of the market.

Qualitative Study (approx. five to eight weeks)

The objective of the first part of the segmentation is to explore and discover the category. Explore consumer needs, why they are using different products etc. Patterns and hypothesis are uncovered during this stage of the research. The findings should give the company information about semiotics and wordings used in the category by consumers. It is not uncommon for consumers to use a very different language to describe how they see the category and the different brands, compared to the internal corporate language.

The output of the qualitative study gives the company insights about the category and summarized results. The qualitative study creates the hypothesis and how to design the quantitative study and the design of the questionnaire.

Quantitative Study (approx. nine to ten weeks)

This part of the research is to verify the qualitative insights gathered in the previous part and quantifying the segment in the category. The size of each segment is quantified in terms of volume and value. The segments are mapped out to see the brands, activities and products used in each of the consumer segments. It creates a holistic overview of the category and provides priorities, recommendations and tools to navigate the category from the consumers' point of view. It is also an excellent tool to spot market gaps and give ideas for future product development.

Implementation and Activation

This part of the research project is about closing the project and presenting the results to key stakeholders. A workshop should be organized again where each function of the company is present. It should also be a forum to develop ideas and write down an action plan for the next steps.

The deeper insights from the qualitative study are combined with more descriptive facts from the quantitative study. The combined results give both an understanding of the underlying motivations and needs of the consumers and a solid document for decision making.

QUALITATIVE RESEARCH

The objective of the qualitative research study is to build an understanding of consumer behavior and needs states in the category. It is used to explore the category and therefore uses exploratory questions to build the framework. In this stage, the project manager only knows roughly what he or she is looking for. The purpose of this stage is to identify, understand, map and group different needs and key drivers in the category.

The data that is gathered here is comprised of words, behavior and images. The goal is to gather this data to enhance the understanding of the category. This step can be described as listening to consumers. Hear their stories and how they navigate the category and let them guide your understanding of the category.

The composition of the focus groups is very important and should be representative of the category. The split of the focus groups should reflect prevalence numbers and regional differences. The consumption behavior normally varies greatly between urban and rural areas of the country. It is not uncommon that highly educated and high-income individuals are overrepresented in major cities in a country.

Consumer preferences can also vary greatly between gender and age. Gender can be a big divider of preferences in a category. Males are often overrepresented for certain brands and vice versa. Age can also divide preferences in a category. Older consumers are often more conservative when it comes to brand choices and tends to switch brands to a lesser extent than younger consumers.

It is up to the project manager to rank what he or she believes is the most appropriate way to set-up the focus groups. It is recommended to put the variables in a spreadsheet to elaborate on the different combinations.

The number of focus groups is also an important factor. The general rule is, the more the better. The absolute minimum number of groups is four for a market segmentation research.

In the below example, three variables are identified as important variables for the category (gender, urbanity and age). With this set-up, it is possible to draw conclusions on differences within these groups and aggregate them. For example, if we look at the preferences of all urban groups vs rural groups, we can analyze the differences in preferences between city and non-city consumers.

Group	Gender	Area	Age	...
1	Females	City	Younger	
2	Females	City	Older	
3	Females	Rural	Younger	
4	Females	Rural	Older	
5	Males	City	Younger	
6	Males	City	Older	
7	Males	Rural	Younger	
8	Males	Rural	Older	

In some categories, it might be more relevant to look at other differences. It could be occasional users vs regular users, occupation, residence, family situation, etc. It is up to the project manager to decide the metrics that are important for the category, based on previous knowledge of the market. It is recommended to present the focus group composition during the initial workshop of the research study.

Duration of the Focus Groups

The duration of the focus groups is of great importance for the depth of data collected from the groups. For a segmentation study, the duration needs to be longer vs other qualitative studies, since it covers a broader spectrum of the market and includes a wide array of brands.

With support from a moderator and stimuli material, the participants will be able to "open up" and talk more in-depth about their thoughts and feelings compared to traditional focus groups. The focus groups need to be in a relaxed environment and have fewer participants than traditional focus groups. The number of participants should be from four to six people. The composition of the groups should be as homogeneous as possible, meaning men and women in separate groups, narrow age spans, people in similar life stages, etc. The needs and category drivers that are creating consumer behavior are identified and mapped out.

The two driving forces that shape human behavior are how we relate to a category relative to ourselves and others. We have a social and personal dimension. On one side of the social dimension, we have individualists who want to be different, want to be seen and feel special. On the opposite side, we have the collective individual that wants to fit in, feel accepted and be part of a community.

On one side of the personal dimension, we have the controlling individual that wants to control the behavior and adhere to a routine. On the opposite side, we have the released individual that enjoy the moment and act on impulse.

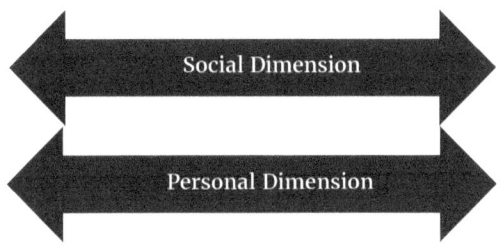

Topics Covered in the Qualitative Questionnaire

Who
Gender, occupation, residence, family and income. Have they used the product recently (screening) do they normally buy it themselves and can they affect the buying decision?

When and Where
When is the product used, at work, leisure with family and children, leisure without children, etc.? How often do the consumers use the product and during what occasion, is it daily, weekly, monthly, etc. Where do they use the product, etc.

What
In which situation they use the product, where did they buy the product? What other products were bought and used when they bought the brand in question.

Why

How would the consumer describe the ideal product for them and what type of personality should it have? How would you feel like when you used the ideal product? What requirements and expectations do you have on the ideal product?

After the initial discussion and spontaneous reactions to these questions, the respondents should be asked about current brands and products in the market. How do they describe the personality of these brands in the market? How do they feel when using this product? What requirements and expectations do they fulfill? The motivational frame of reference is then developed based on the ideal product and its attributes (not predetermined).

The segments are mapped out on top of the attributes and assigned descriptive names. The names of the different segments should be descriptive of the attributes and easy to understand when communicating the findings to the organization. This is also an exercise that is important to do together with internal stakeholders to align the findings of the research at the mid-point of the segmentation process.

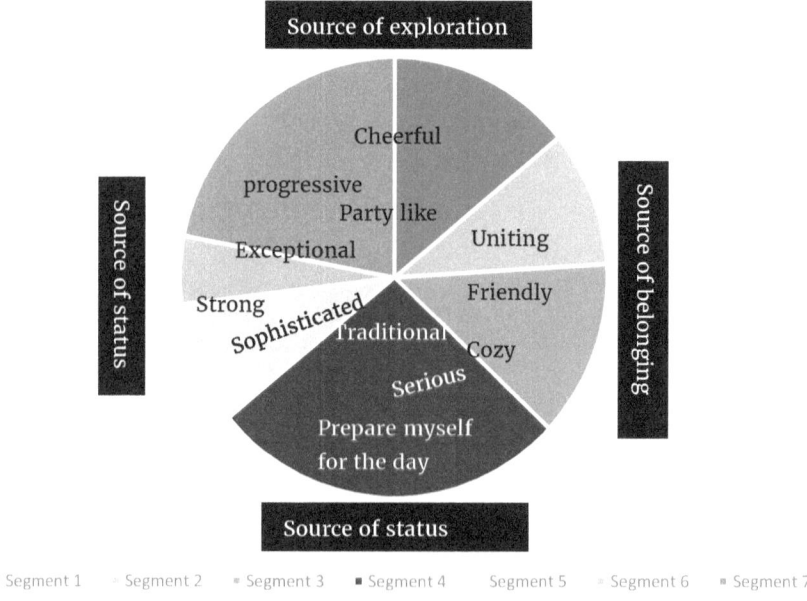

Every segment can then be profiled based on who they are and how they would like their ideal product to be. The segments are now the new internal language of the company when the organization describes its customer base.

QUANTITATIVE RESEARCH

The objective of the quantitative study is to quantify the findings discovered in the qualitative phase of the research project. The study should be conducted via a web panel with a national representative sample, based on gender, age and region. The screening process gives valuable insights about penetration in the category for the specific target group in the population.

A list of brands should be provided to the research company. The recommended sample size is 1 500 respondents or more. It is of great importance for the implementation of the psychographic and needs-based segmentation that location data (example zip-codes) is gathered in the quantitative study. This will be used in the market segmentation model outlined in the next chapter.

All the relevant attributes found in the qualitative study should be incorporated into the questionnaire at this stage. These include emotional benefits, product benefits, personality and social identity.

Some of the consumer segments identified in the qualitative study might need to be merged if it turns out that the size of one segment is not significant enough in terms of volume and value. It needs to make sense for the company to target a consumer segment.

The results from the quantitative study should cover the exact size of each consumer segment in terms of both volume and profitability. The quantitative study gives the size of the consumer segments in percent, which is then multiplied with the volume and profit pool to get volume and profitability data. This information is then presented to the organization and used for product development, brand positioning and marketing messages.

IMPLEMENTATION OF MARKET SEGMENTATION

Bring It all together
Part 3

UTILIZATION OF DATA

The implementation phase is different for each company depending on the available data and the goal of the market segmentation. It is up to the company to decide what kind of variables that are important for the brand portfolio, but the framework remains the same. The framework and how to build the market segmentation model are outlined below.

Zip-Codes	**Psychographics**	• Need states • Ideal product • Position/ Image • Type of usage
	Density	• Super Urban • Urban • Town • Sub Urban • Rural
	Demographics	• Gender • Ethnicity • Education • Occupation • Income
Geo-data		Point databases, areas of special interest (University, airports, bars etc.)
Sales data		• Store locations • Sales volumes • Capital equipment • Etc.
Company Knowledge		• Market Knowledge • Brand Priorities • Surveys • Etc.

All available data needs to be classified and imported to a mapping program to make calculations necessary for the market segmentation model.

Brand Criteria's

The implementation phase starts with the definition of the exact target group for the company's portfolio of brands. This is the base of the market segmentation implementation. This is an extensive exercise where the marketing department and management team normally sit together to define the target groups. The targets are based on the current consumer profile of the brand and the long-term aspirational plan within the next three to five years. All variables above can be used to formulate the brand criteria.

Each variable is assigned a weight from 0% to 100%. The higher the weight, the more important the variable becomes in the market segmentation model. Below is an example of how the brand criteria might look like.

University cities are considered an important variable for brand C in this example. The segmentation is not limited to just university cities. If the company believes that airports or train stations are important for a brand, this can easily be incorporated into the model.

		Brand A	Weight %	SUB TOTAL	Brand B	Weight %	SUB TOTAL	Brand C	Weight %	SUB TOTAL
Internal	Price Segment:	Premium	5%	10%	.		0%	Value	10%	10%
Demographic	Urbanity	Urban, Super Urban	20%		Rural	30%		Exurban, Town	20%	
	Age	25-45 years	10%		45-65+ years	30%		18-44 years	10%	
	Income level	Mid-Low, High	15%		.			Low, High	20%	
	Education	Post_Secondary	20%	80%	Primary		90%	Primary, Secondary	15%	75%
	Ethnicity	.			Hispanic			.		
	Occupation	White Collar	15%		Blue Collar	30%		.		
	University City	.			.			Yes	5%	
	Gender	.			.			Male	5%	
Psychographics	Segment 1	.			.			Target		
	Segment 2	Target			Target			.		
	Segment 3	Target			.			.		
	Segment 4	.		10%	.		10%	Target		15%
	Segment 5	.			.			.		
	Segment 6	.			.			.		
	Segment 7	.			.			.		
	TOTAL WEIGHT:			100%			100%			100%

Demographic Data

One of the great benefits of demographic data is that it is normally easily available across many countries. Particularly North America and Europe benefit from very detailed demographic information down to state, county, municipal areas, zip-code, etc. This wealth of data can be utilized for targeting specific consumer groups and market the right brand in the right locations to the right consumers.

Demographic data is normally available for free on government sites or available to be purchased for a relatively low cost in most countries. Demographic data unlocks value beyond just beautiful data visualizations on maps.

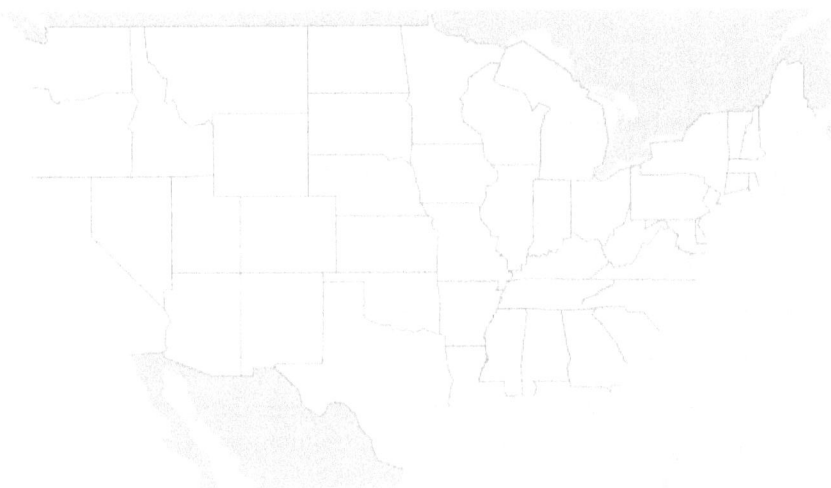

Source: https://data.census.gov/

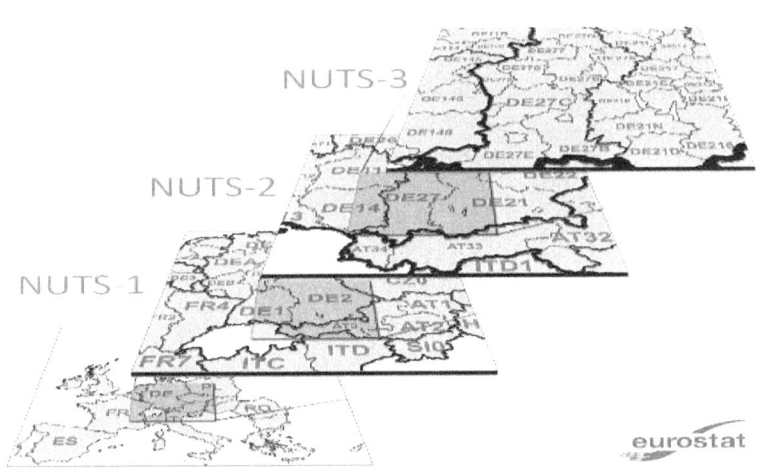

Source: https://ec.europa.eu/eurostat

Store Locations

FMCG companies normally rely to a high extent on traditional store locations to promote and sell their products. It is not uncommon for an FMCG company to have a database with the coordinates for all stores in the country it operates in. This data can also be gathered by sales representatives when visiting customers in the country.

The longitude and latitude data can be used in various mapping programs to pinpoint each store location in the country. This forms the second layer in the market segmentation model.

Density Classification

Density is often an important factor to determine the buying preferences of consumers. Density also an important factor when estimating how far a consumer is willing to travel to reach a specific store and if consumers are expected to drive or walk to a store. At this stage, it is good to invite Area Sales Managers and Sales Representatives to discuss general rules of how consumers reach stores in different areas.

General assumptions are that consumers in higher density areas are less willing to travel to reach their store destination. Consumers normally prefer to walk to the store in urban areas. In rural areas, consumers are expected to drive to reach their destination. Below is an example of how the classifications are made. This is the foundation for defining trade areas that will be explained later in this chapter.

Density Classifications

- Super Urban -2 min walk time
- Urban – 5 min walk time
- Town – 10 min walk time
- Sub/Ex-urban 5 min Drive time
- Rural – 10 min drive time

Volume/Sales Classifications

Sales or volumes for a store play an important role to determine the general attractiveness of a store. In the segmentation, the volumes are used as a proxy to tell how competitive a store is relative to other stores in proximity. High store sales add driving time to the density classifications. Consumers are expected to travel a longer distance to reach a supermarket vs a grocery store.

Below is an example of how sales add driving time per density class

- Super Urban +/- 0 min
- Urban +/- 2 min
- Town +/- 3 min
- Sub/ Ex-urban +/- 2 min (drive time)
- Rural +/- 5 min (drive time)

+ if weekly sales exceed >400 000 USD
0, if weekly sales between 250 000 – 399 999 USD
-, if weekly sales below <250 000

Age Classification

Aggregation of different age groups is common practice in many industries and there are many standardized ways to calculate it. The most popular one is to classify it per generation: Generation Z (Teens and younger), Millennial (18-34 years old), Gen X (35-50 years old), Boomer (50-70 years old) and Silent (+70 years old).

It is important that the age groups are relevant for the company in terms of brand positioning. There are no limitations in the number of age groups that can be used in the market segmentation model.

Below is an example of age categorization that can be used in the market segmentation

- 0-17 years old
- 18-24 years old
- 25-34 Years old
- 35-44 years old
- 45-54 years old
- 55-64 years old
- +65 years Old

Income Classification

There are several ways of classifying income in the market. A recommended approach is to have four classifications for income for the market segmentation model. Income data is generally easily available on an aggregated level. The starting point should be to identify the median income in the market and then proceed to calculate the quartiles. This approach divides the income groups into four equal parts and can be visualized in a boxplot diagram. It is not unusual for demographic data to already contain income classifications.

The four classifications
- Low income
- Mid-Low income
- Mid-High Income
- High Income

Road Networks and Speed Limitations

This layer is of great importance for the implementation of the market segmentation. By understanding the road networks and the speed limits for each road, we gain a good understanding of how long it will take to reach different store locations in the country. This data is also widely available and can either be accessed for free or at a low cost. Speed limitations and road networks are used every time you use a mapping program such as Google maps. This information is of great value to the implementation of the market segmentation.

Trade Areas

The layers are starting to come together, and you are sitting on a wealth of information to be used for your market segmentation.

Many mapping programs provide you with tools to calculate how far you can travel within certain time limits. By applying the above information to each store in the market, you can start to calculate the trade areas for each store based on the coordinates that have been gathered.

Density Classes for Trade Areas

In city areas with high density, most people are assumed to walk to their store to get their products. In other more rural locations, consumers are assumed to drive to their store to get their products. It is up to the company to decide depending on the country and density, how likely it is for a consumer to walk/drive to its destination. It is also important to make assumptions about how far a pedestrian or a car owner is willing to walk/drive to reach its destination.

The average speed of a pedestrian is about 3.1 miles per hour / 5 kilometres per hour. By using the store location and your mapping tool, you can draw the trade area of the store by calculating how far you can walk in for example 3 minutes in every direction (North, East, South, West).

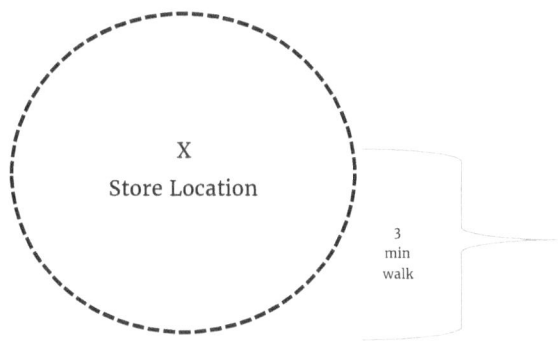

The same principle applies to customers that drive, but the exception here is that you use the speed limits of the road networks to determine how far you can drive in 5, 10, 15 min, etc. The mapping program will use the road networks to calculate how far you can drive in 10 min in each direction and this forms to trade area for driving.

Extrapolate the Results from the Quantitative Study

The last layer to add to the mapping program is the results of the quantitative research. As mentioned in the previous section, it is important to have enough sample size in order to perform this analysis.

In the quantitative research, the zip-codes were gathered from each respondent. This valuable information is then used to extrapolate the data to the total population and geography. The purpose of the exercise is to anchor the number of induvial for each segment to zip-code level in the market.

The analysis process contains three steps
1. The total population data is joined with the quantitative survey through the common denominator, zip-codes. Both data sources need to contain the same type of information for this to work.
2. Each zip-code get a distribution of individuals in each of the identified segments. This is possible as the data collected in the survey is representative for the overall market.
3. Statistical inference is used to apply the survey results to the whole market.

The analysis and statistical model used in this step is called scoring analysis.

Segment	Original Distribution	Estimated Distribution	Variance	Hit Rate
Segment 1	14%	15.9%	1.9%	83%
Segment 2	10%	10.9%	0.9%	82.6%
Segment 3	13%	12.6%	−0.4%	89.6%
Segment 4	27%	26.1%	−0.9%	78.9%
Segment 5	9%	8.5%	−0.5%	75.8%
Segment 6	5%	5.3%	0.3%	79.4%
Segment 7	22%	20.7%	−1.3%	92.8%

Zip-Code	Area	Segment 1	Segment 2	Segment 3	Segment 4	Segment 5	Segment 6	Segment 7
33124	Miami	245	179	176	201	464	176	221
33125	Miami	99	55	452	479	301	132	315
33126	Miami	409	500	93	66	219	396	305
33127	Miami	262	407	67	83	356	410	433
33128	Miami	216	411	287	191	431	428	272
33129	Miami	274	279	471	75	303	114	189
33130	Miami	478	162	81	103	45	66	391
33131	Miami	192	439	468	278	52	498	393
33132	Miami	386	64	377	254	106	155	369

33133	Miami	232	278	245	330	120	66	181
33134	Miami	392	442	463	18	27	166	276
33135	Miami	273	311	323	81	122	142	285
33136	Miami	291	311	487	412	17	356	177

The next step is to calculate the share of users per zip-code in the analysis. This is simply done by dividing the segmentation results per zip-code with the total population to get the share of product users. The highest number of users per segment becomes the dominant segment in the respective areas. In the first zip-code, segment 5 is the most prevalent segment in the area.

WEIGHTED GEO-SEGMENTATION MODEL

Once the demographic and psychographic data is aggregated for each retail outlet in the market, it is time to assign a brand or SKU focus for each retail outlet in the market.

A statistical method (z-score model) is used to normalize and combining all data sets based on the brands' target criteria and associated weights per brand. The z-score model calculates how well a specific trade area corresponds to the pre-defined brand criteria. For example, income and educational level. A higher Z-score indicates that it is a good fit for the brand.

$$Z = (\chi - \mu)/\sigma$$

χ is the raw score to be standardized
μ is the mean of the total population
σ is the standard deviation of the population

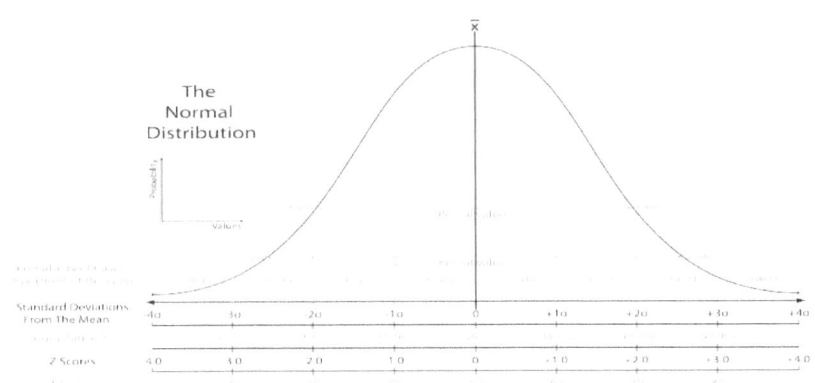

The
Normal
Distribution

Standard Deviations
From The Mean

Z Scores

Calculating the Scores

The first step is to convert the data for each retail outlet/account code in the market from absolute numbers to percentage. We are interested in the number of people as a percent of the total population in a certain trade area that is between 18 and 24 years old. All variables that we have identified as important, are aggregated to a trade area. For location data such as University areas, these are coded as zero or one. If there is a university within the trade area of a store, it gets the value 1 and vice versa. The psychographic segments are calculated slightly differently from other variables. If 100% of a store's trade area falls within segment 1, then the value becomes 100%. If 50% of the psychographic segment falls within the trade areas, it gets the value 50% and so on.

Account Code	% 18–25 year of age	Super Urban / Urban	Mid–High Education	White Collar	University	Premium Share	Segment 1 or 4
AC001432	19.5%	18.6%	57.1%	66.4%	0.0%	68.3%	0.0%
AC001353	12.1%	28.4%	46.2%	55.4%	0.0%	79.2%	0.0%
AC005931	11.1%	0.0%	17.8%	43.5%	0.0%	50.1%	0.0%
AC003951	11.2%	0.0%	27.8%	61.3%	0.0%	34.4%	100.0%

Code							
AC0095 36	12.4%	0.0%	44.0%	64.0%	0.0%	70.5%	100.0%
AC0015 32	12.1%	10.6%	29.6%	48.8%	0.0%	10.9%	0.0%
AC0013 55	12.0%	12.7%	34.1%	49.4%	0.0%	63.4%	0.0%
AC0059 11	11.9%	50.1%	43.0%	61.3%	0.0%	22.5%	0.0%
AC0039 35	10.7%	0.0%	21.4%	56.0%	0.0%	91.6%	0.0%
AC0095 56	16.6%	31.6%	41.6%	55.8%	100.0%	27.1%	0.0%
AC0012 35	12.5%	0.0%	25.1%	52.7%	0.0%	85.0%	0.0%
AC0013 38	10.0%	23.9%	28.5%	48.7%	0.0%	55.6%	100.0%
AC0052 35	10.2%	53.0%	50.8%	70.8%	0.0%	98.3%	0.0%
AC0082 53	10.7%	87.6%	55.2%	69.4%	0.0%	24.3%	0.0%
AC0019 71	11.5%	98.2%	60.9%	65.8%	0.0%	72.4%	0.0%

For each of the variables, we calculate the mean, standard deviation and add the weights that were determined per brand in the previous steps.

Mean	12.57%	35.18%	37.26%	55.67%	12.93%	56.90%	20.00%
SD	3.75%	38.74%	14.27%	9.47%	33.55%	6.58%	28.58%
Weight (Brand)	15.0%	20.0%	20.0%	10.0%	5.0%	10.0%	20.0%

The next step is to calculate the Z-Score for each of the variables that we have in the table.

Z-Score (% 18-25)	Z-Score (SU/U)	Z-Score (Mid-High Edu)	Z-Score (White C)	Z-Score (Uni)	Z-Score (Prem Share)	Z-Score (PS)
1.84	-0.43	1.39	1.13	-0.39	1.74	-0.70
-0.12	-0.17	0.63	-0.03	-0.39	3.39	-0.70
-0.39	-0.91	-1.37	-1.29	-0.39	-1.04	-0.70

-0.36	-0.91	-0.67	0.59	-0.39	-3.42	2.80
-0.05	-0.91	0.47	0.88	-0.39	2.06	2.80
-0.12	-0.63	-0.53	-0.72	-0.39	-6.99	-0.70
-0.14	-0.58	-0.22	-0.66	-0.39	0.99	-0.70
-0.17	0.39	0.40	0.60	-0.39	-5.24	-0.70
-0.50	-0.91	-1.11	0.03	-0.39	5.28	-0.70
1.07	-0.09	0.30	0.01	2.60	-4.54	-0.70
-0.01	-0.91	-0.85	-0.31	-0.39	4.27	-0.70
-0.68	-0.29	-0.62	-0.74	-0.39	-0.19	2.80
-0.64	0.46	0.95	1.60	-0.39	6.29	-0.70
-0.49	1.35	1.26	1.45	-0.39	-4.96	-0.70
-0.27	1.63	1.65	1.07	-0.39	2.36	-0.70

Total Score is per account code is calculated by multiplying the Z-Score with the corresponding weight per variable. This results in a total Z-Score for all our variables in the table.

Overview of the Total Calculation

Account Code	% 18-25 year of age	Super Urban / Urban	Mid-High Education	White Collar	University	Premium Share	Segment 1 or 4	Z-Score (% 18-25)	Z-Score (SU/U)	Z-Score (Mid-High Edu)	Z-Score (White C)	Z-Score (Uni)	Z-Score (Prem Share)	Z-Score (PS)	Total Score
Mean	12.57%	35.18%	37.26%	55.67%	12.93%	47.96%	20.00%								
SD	3.75%	38.74%	14.27%	9.47%	33.55%	6.58%	28.58%								
Weight (Brand)	15.0%	20.0%	20.0%	10.0%	5.0%	10.0%	20.0%								
...	...	...	...	...	...	...	...	...	...	...	...	...	...	...	...
AC001971	11.5%	98.2%	60.9%	65.8%	0.0%	65.4%	0.0%	-0.27	1.63	1.65	1.07	-0.39	2.64	-0.70	0.97
AC008253	10.7%	87.6%	55.2%	69.4%	0.0%	59.2%	0.0%	-0.49	1.35	1.26	1.45	-0.39	1.71	-0.70	0.75
AC005235	10.2%	53.0%	50.8%	70.8%	0.0%	59.4%	0.0%	-0.64	0.46	0.95	1.60	-0.39	1.74	-0.70	0.50
AC000338	10.0%	23.9%	28.5%	48.7%	0.0%	65.5%	0.0%	-0.68	-0.29	-0.62	-0.74	-0.39	2.67	-0.70	-0.11
AC000235	12.5%	0.0%	25.1%	52.7%	0.0%	31.4%	0.0%	-0.01	-0.91	-0.85	-0.31	-0.39	-2.52	-0.70	-0.66
AC009556	16.6%	31.6%	41.6%	55.8%	100.0%	72.7%	0.0%	1.07	-0.09	0.30	0.01	2.60	3.76	-0.70	0.71
AC003935	10.7%	0.0%	21.4%	56.0%	0.0%	87.7%	0.0%	-0.50	-0.91	-1.11	0.03	-0.39	6.05	-0.70	0.11
AC005911	11.9%	50.1%	43.0%	61.3%	0.0%	35.9%	0.0%	-0.17	0.39	0.40	0.60	-0.39	-1.83	-0.70	-0.01
AC000355	12.0%	12.7%	34.1%	49.4%	0.0%	52.0%	0.0%	-0.14	-0.58	-0.22	-0.66	-0.39	0.61	-0.70	-0.21
AC000532	12.1%	10.6%	29.6%	48.8%	0.0%	10.1%	0.0%	-0.12	-0.63	-0.53	-0.72	-0.39	-5.75	-0.70	-0.92
AC009536	12.4%	0.0%	44.0%	64.0%	0.0%	0.5%	100.0%	-0.05	-0.91	0.47	0.88	-0.39	-7.22	2.80	-0.75
AC003951	11.2%	0.0%	27.8%	61.3%	0.0%	47.1%	100.0%	-0.36	-0.91	-0.67	0.59	-0.39	-0.13	2.80	-0.34
AC005931	11.1%	0.0%	17.8%	43.5%	0.0%	55.0%	0.0%	-0.39	-0.91	-1.37	-1.29	-0.39	1.07	-0.70	-0.55
AC003353	12.1%	28.4%	46.2%	55.4%	0.0%	7.8%	0.0%	-0.12	-0.17	0.63	-0.03	-0.39	-6.10	-0.70	-0.56
AC004432	19.5%	18.6%	57.1%	66.4%	0.0%	69.7%	0.0%	1.84	-0.43	1.39	1.13	-0.39	3.31	-0.70	0.89

Brand Priority

In order to ensure that only one brand ends up as the focus for the retail outlet, a priority list of brands needs to be established. This is to ensure that each store has one priority and one secondary brand priority. This is imported from the brand criteria.

Brand	Prioritization
Brand A	First priority
Brand B	Second priority
Brand C	Third priority

Ranking the Scores

After we have normalized the results and calculated the total Z-Score per account, we then proceed to rank the account codes from 1 to the last observation in the dataset for each of the brands. Remember that the higher the Z-score, the better fit for the brand.

Account Code	Brand A		Brand B		Brand C	
	Rank	Total Score	Rank	Total Score	Rank	Total Score
AC005623	1	3.550	1192	0.811	15277	−0.754
AC008345	2	3.413	16357	−1.408	16353	−1.347
AC001794	3	3.408	12412	−0.345	15242	−0.746
AC004673	4	3.383	7622	0.011	15625	−0.852
AC002567	5	3.309	373	1.238	12577	−0.327
AC002325	6	3.269	1509	0.715	10599	−0.134
AC007937	7	3.260	154	1.456	6434	0.156
AC001678	8	3.201	16224	−1.228	16287	−1.221
AC006953	9	3.147	13660	−0.478	15842	−0.935
AC003579	10	3.084	136	1.485	7854	0.064
AC002334	11	2.976	10896	−0.222	12576	−0.327
AC004845	12	2.937	476	1.168	4546	0.278

...	...	...	...	...	...	...

After the ranks have been calculated, it is divided into 18 different groups. The number of groups is up to the company to decide. A larger number of stores require more groups.

In this example, we have ranked the stores from Top 500, Top 501-1000 and so on. This gives a measurement of importance from 1 to 18.

Account Code	Brand A	Brand B	Brand C	PRIM	SEC	Check	PRIM brand	SEC brand
AC001432	13	6	12	6	12	Ok	B	C
AC001353	2	18	9	2	9	Ok	A	C
AC005931	5	9	5	5	5	#2	A	C
AC003951	17	14	11	11	14	Ok	C	B
AC009536	9	11	7	7	9	Ok	C	A

For each account, the brand with the lowest number is the one that becomes the primary brand focus in the store. The brand with the second-lowest number gets assigned the secondary brand focus.

For the Account Code AC005931, we end up with the same score for brand A and C. This is where the brand priority comes into force. Since the market has valued brand A as more important than brand C, Brand A becomes the primary brand focus in the store.

These calculations can be done in any spreadsheet program or via statistical programs.

Bringing it All Together

Once all layers have been applied in the mapping program and the trade areas have been calculated, it is now time to determine what brand communication should be used in each store.

		Count of all Outlets		% of Outlets	
	Brand	Primary	Secondary	Primary	Secondary
Visited Stores	Brand A	33,405	33,405	44.4%	44.4%
	Brand B	28,000	28,000	37.2%	37.2%
	Brand C	13,837	13,837	18.4%	18.4%
	Total	**75,242**	**75,242**	**100.0%**	**100.0%**
Non–Visited Stores	Brand A	20,345	20,345	29.4%	29.4%
	Brand B	32,994	32,994	47.6%	47.6%
	Brand C	15,954	15,954	23.0%	23.0%
	Total	**69,293**	**69,293**	**100.0%**	**100.0%**

How to Utilize the Market Segmentation Model

There are many ways for a company to utilize the market segmentation model. The most common way is to promote a specific brand in a store. This allows a company to focus its market efforts on multiple brands instead of a single brand focus nationally.

Depending on the products and categories the company operates in, the market segmentation can be used in several ways. If a company is in the beverage industry where its products are sold in refrigerators, the company can use this market segmentation to brand the cooler with its primary brand focus. The market segmentation model identifies the brand as the most likely to sell in a specific store.

If the company sells shampoo products, the market segmentation can be used to put up the point of sales material on the shelves to promote the brand that is most likely to sell in a specific store.

The next step of the market segmentation is to adapt planograms according to the brand that is most likely to sell in specific locations. This not only promotes the right brand in the right store but also mitigates the risk of an out of stock situation. If the market segmentation has shown that brand A is the most suitable brand for a store location, then the planogram should be adapted so that brand A receives the highest number of faces in the planogram. A company can with the market segmentation have multiple standardized planograms for each of the brand focus areas.

Not limited to Brands

The market segmentation model can also be used for SKU prioritization or when launching a new product. The company can run the segmentation model and instead of completing all the steps, stop at the store ranking step. This gives the market a list of all the top stores that are most suitable for a product launch. A company that wants to have distribution in the top 3000 stores can easily use the segmentation model for this purpose.

Monitoring and Evaluating

As with all models and strategies, the market segmentation model should be evaluated on an ongoing basis. The best way to do this is to import all accounts with the primary and secondary brand focus in an internal database system and monitor the results against stores that have a different brand focus. If the initial criteria for the brand are suitable and fitting for the target group, the primary brand focus in these outlets should perform significantly better vs outlets with a different brand focus. The brand criteria can be fine-tuned along the way to provide an optimal position of the brand.

The market segmentation model for brands and SKUs can easily be combined as well. Brand segmentation can dictate the brand hero for a store and the SKU segmentation can be used for prioritizing different SKUs within a specific brand family.

The market segmentation model has a proven successful track record in the FMCG industry and by offering the right brand, in the right store to the right consumers, the FMCG company becomes a true consumer-centric organization.

ABOUT THE AUTHOR

Mark Freeman is the author of the book Market Segmentation in the FMCG Industry and for multiple articles published on the topic.

Mark has a financial educational background and over 10 years of experience working in the retail and FMCG industry. He has held various responsibilities in Marketing and Sales throughout the years, in both local and global roles.

Mark is passionate about marketing and discovered early on how powerful a market segmentation tool can be for a company. It unlocks the true potential in the market and creates insights and durable competitive advantages for a company.

Through extensive research about market segmentation, it was a surprise to find that so few books focus on the subject. Most of the books are also written by academic professionals and not by practitioners. The knowledge shared in Mark's book is meant to be a step-by-step guide of market segmentation. The objective was to give the readers tools and guidance of how to successfully lead market segmentation projects. It is a book to kick-start a career within the FMCG industry.

NEVER STOP LEARNING

A final request: Please review this book on Amazon

If you have read this far, I want to extend my profound thank you. It was a true pleasure to write this book. When you have a spare moment, I would appreciate your honest review and opinion about the Market Segmentation in the FMCG Industry **book on Amazon.**